Bible Puzzler #1

based on stories from Matthew's Gospel

CSS Publishing Company, Inc., Lima, Ohio

BIBLE PUZZLER #1

Reprinted in 2002

Copyright © 1985 by
CSS Publishing Company, Inc.
Lima, Ohio

The original purchaser may photocopy material in this publication for use as it was intended (i.e., worship material for worship use; educational material for classroom use; dramatic material for staging or production). No additional permission is required from the publisher for such copying by the original purchaser only. Inquiries should be addressed to: Permissions, CSS Publishing Company, Inc., P.O. Box 4503, Lima, Ohio 45802-4503.

For more information about CSS Publishing Company resources, visit our website at www.csspub.com or e-mail us at custserv@csspub.com or call (800) 241-4056.

ISBN 0-89536-741-6   PRINTED IN U.S.A.

This Puzzle Book Belongs To

Who Received It From

What a Birth

Matthew 1:18-25

Mary and Joseph were an ordinary Jewish couple engaged to be married. One day something happened that caused Joseph all kinds of worry. Mary was told by an angel that she was to be the mother of a baby by the power of the Holy Spirit! That was wonderful news for Mary — but not very easy to explain to Joseph. He didn't know what to do. Finally, Joseph decided to quietly break the engagement, but before he could do anything, he had a dream. In his dream an angel said: "Joseph ... do not be afraid to take Mary to be your wife. For it is by the Holy Spirit that she is going to have a baby. She will have a son, and you will name him Jesus because he will save his people from their sins."

WORD SCRAMBLE. These words got all mixed up! Try to unscramble them and write them in the spaces provided.

1. OSEJPH
2. ONS
3. ARMY
4. TIRSPI

Announcement

A MARY-JOSEPH PUZZLE FOR YOU. Can you figure out the answers to this puzzle? You might get some help from today's lesson.

Across
1. Today's lesson is all about a young couple named Mary and _ _ _ _ _ _.
2. The name "Jesus" means "he will save the people from their _ _ _ _."
3. In a dream Joseph learned that Mary was to have a _ _ _.
4. To _ _ _ _ his people from sin, Jesus died on the cross.
5. A _ _ _ _ _ is a very holy, good person.

Down
1. Joseph found out in a dream that Mary's baby would be named _ _ _ _ _.
2. _ _ _ _ might be falling on Jesus' birthday.
6. All of this happened to Mary by the power of the Holy _ _ _ _ _ _.
7. An _ _ _ _ _ told Mary she would have a son.
8. Joseph was told not to be afraid to take Mary to be _ _ _ wife.

Wise Men Still

Matthew 2:1-12

The Magi were wise men from the East who had been studying and following the stars. They were led to Jerusalem where they asked this question: "Where is the baby born to be the king of the Jews?" This question upset everyone, especially King Herod. He called his wise men together and asked them what they knew about this "king." They told him that the child would be born in Bethlehem of Judah. So Herod told the Magi what the teachers had said. He asked them to come back if they found the child — because he wanted to worship him also. When the kings found the child and his parents, they were very happy. They gave him wonderful gifts. Then they went back to their homes in the East.

WORD SCRAMBLE. These words from today's story got all mixed up. Try to unscramble them and write them in the spaces provided.

1. INGKS
2. IGFTS
3. AGMI
4. ERODH
5. ASTE
6. EWJS
7. ABYB

Adore Him

A WISE-MEN PUZZLE. Most of the answers to this puzzle can be found in today's story about the Magi. Try to solve it!

Across
1. The _ _ _ _ were men from far away who came seeking the king of the Jews.
2. These wise men had studied and followed the _ _ _ _ _.
3. King _ _ _ _ _ was very upset by the wise men's questions.

Down
4. The star led the wise men to the city of _ _ _ _ _ _ _ _ _.
5. The king's own wise men told him that the baby would be _ _ _ _ in Bethlehem of Judah.
6. After the Magi saw the child, they went back to their homes in the _ _ _ _.
7. "We Three Kings" is a Christmas _ _ _ _ which tells the story of the Magi.

A King Who

Matthew 2:13-15, 19-23

Even when Jesus was a baby, his life was in danger. The Gospel story tells us that King Herod was very worried about this baby who was supposed to become the king of the Jews. The teachers and wise men told him that the

A WORD SCRAMBLE. These words from today's story got all mixed up. Try to unscramble them in the spaces provided.

1. ILFE
2. HOERD
3. ISEW
4. GPYTE
5. THAZANER
6. AYBB
7. OSEJPH

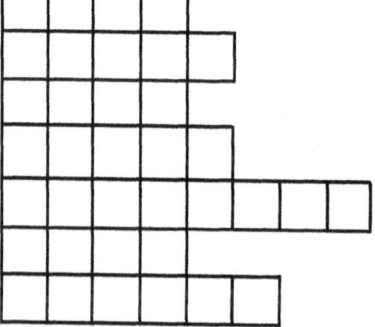

Went Crazy

baby would be born in Bethlehem of Judah. So Herod decided to get rid of all the baby boys living in that area. But Jesus escaped because Joseph was warned in a dream to take Mary and the child into the land of Egypt. This is where they lived until King Herod died. Then they came back and settled in the town of Nazareth.

HIDDEN MESSAGE. A special message has been hidden for you in the letters and numbers below. Just follow the number one until you find a word. Do the same for two, three, and so on until you can write the whole message in the space below.

1	3	8	2	8	2	9	4	2	5	4	9	5
M	A	I	J	N	O	E	J	S	H	E	G	I
1	3	9	4	2	4	1	6	7	9	6	2	
A	N	Y	S	E	U	R	F	H	P	R	P	
5	4	6	6	7	9	7	3	1	7	2	7	
D	S	O	M	E	T	R	D	Y	O	H	D	

Write the message here: _____

_____

Noisy in

Matthew 3:1-12

Before Jesus began his work on this earth, his cousin John helped the people get ready for him. John was really a sight to see! He began preaching in the desert — "Turn away from your sins because the kingdom of heaven is near!" John wore clothes made of camel's hair and had a leather belt around his waist. His food was locusts and wild honey. People came from all over the countryside to hear him preach. Those who were sorry for their sins were baptized by John in the Jordan River. That is why he became known as John the Baptizer.

A JOHN THE BAPTIZER PUZZLE. All the answers to this puzzle can be found in today's lesson about John the Baptizer. Try to solve it without looking back!

Across
1. The name of Jesus's cousin. _ _ _ _
2. All who were sorry for their _ _ _ _ were baptized.
3. John wore clothes made from camel's _ _ _ _.
4. John's message was, "_ _ _ _ away from your sins ..."
5. John baptized people in the _ _ _ _ _ _ River.
6. John had a lot of things to _ _ _ about the kingdom of heaven.

Down
7. Jesus' cousin lived in the _ _ _ _ _ _.
8. John ate locusts and wild _ _ _ _ _.
9. Jesus was a relative of John — his _ _ _ _ _ _.
10. John's job was to help people get _ _ _ _ _ for Jesus.

the Desert

In the space below, write the message which John the Baptizer preached to all the people.

Fighting With

Matthew 4:1-11

Before Jesus began his preaching and teaching, the Spirit led him into the desert for forty days of prayer and fasting. After all that time, Jesus was probably tired and hungry. The devil knew this because he tried to tempt Jesus. First he said, "Turn these stones into bread, if you are really God's Son!" But Jesus refused, saying that God's word was his food. Then the

WORD SCRAMBLE. These words got all mixed up. Try to figure them out — you might get some help from today's story. Then write them in the space provided.

1. PIRTIS
2. EVDIL
3. ETTLAB
4. ESJUS
5. ESERTD
6. PTEMT

the Devil

devil took Jesus to the top of the Temple and said, "If you are God's Son, prove it by throwing yourself down. God will send his angels to catch you." But Jesus said, "Do not put the Lord your God to the test!" Finally, the devil took Jesus way up to a high mountain where he could see all the beauty of the earth. He told Jesus he would give all of this to him, if Jesus would just worship him. Jesus finally got rid of the devil when he said, "Go away, Satan!" Jesus won the battle with the devil.

HIDDEN WORDS. These words are hiding in the letters below. They are going up, down, forward, backward, and even diagonally. Circle the ones you find.

Words									
Jesus	J	E	S	U	S	A	B	C	M
Spirit	S	T	R	E	S	E	D	D	O
Desert									
Forty	P	F	S	E	N	O	T	S	U
Prayer									
Fasting	I	A	O	E	F	G	H	D	N
Bread	R	S	E	R	V	E	I	A	T
Stones									
Mountain	I	T	J	H	T	R	A	E	A
Serve	T	I	P	R	A	Y	E	R	I
Earth									
Hungry	K	N	F	O	O	D	S	B	N
Food									
	C	G	H	U	N	G	R	Y	D

13

What a

Matthew 4:12-23

When Jesus began his public life, he chose special people — disciples — to help him with his work. This is how it happened. One day he was walking along the shore of Lake Galilee. There he saw two brothers who were fishermen — Simon (called Peter) and Andrew. They were catching fish in the lake with a net. Jesus looked at them and said, "Come with me and I will teach you to catch men." Simon Peter and Andrew left their boat and

HIDDEN WORDS. Can you find these words from today's story hiding in the letters below? Remember, you might see them hiding up, down, forward, backward, and even diagonally. Circle the ones you find.

Words									
Public									
James	P	E	T	E	R	A	B	D	F
Jesus	U	J	E	S	U	S	W	I	O
Andrew									
Brothers	B	J	N	J	B	C	E	S	L
Lake	L	A	K	E	O	D	R	C	L
Boat									
Peter	I	M	E	F	A	H	D	I	O
John									
Galilee	C	E	G	H	T	I	N	P	W
Disciples	J	S	K	R	O	W	A	L	K
Follow									
Net	G	A	L	I	L	E	E	E	L
Work	B	R	O	T	H	E	R	S	M

Catch!

nets and followed him. Then Jesus saw James and John. They were in their boat with their father getting ready to go fishing. Jesus said to them, "Come, follow me." James and John left their father and followed him right away. These were the first disciples of Jesus.

HIDDEN MESSAGE. There is a message hidden in the numbers and letters below. Just follow the number one until you form a word. Do the same for all of the other numbers, then write the message in the space below.

2	6	1	7	3	4	5	1
S	G	J	T	T	D	W	E
6	3	4	8	2	7	4	5
O	H	I	C	A	O	S	E
6	1	8	5	4	5	1	2
I	S	A	R	C	E	U	I
6	4	8	6	3	8	4	9
N	I	T	G	E	C	P	M
4	1	9	4	9	8	4	2
L	S	E	E	N	H	S	D

Write the message here: _____

_____

How to

Matthew 5:1-12

One day Jesus gave a wonderful sermon to lots of people. He went up a hill and everyone sat around him. Jesus started his sermon by telling them who would be "blessed" or "happy" — in other words, who would be the saints — the people who would get to heaven. Can you guess who they were?

WORD SCRAMBLE. These words from today's story got all mixed up. Try to unscramble them and write them in the space provided.

1. EB
2. ILLH
3. NEO
4. AINTSS
5. ERMONS
6. ERA
7. OD

Be a Saint

Jesus said the "happy" ones are the poor in spirit, those who are sad; those who are humble, merciful, pure in heart; those who do what God wants; those who work for peace; those who suffer because they are God's followers. Are you one of God's "holy" people?

HIDDEN WORDS. These words from today's story are hiding in the letters below. They might be going up or down, forward or backward, or even diagonally. Circle the ones you find.

Sermon									
Lots	S	E	R	M	O	N	J	D	F	S
People	A	A	L	L	I	H	E	E	O	A
Jesus	L	O	T	S	B	C	S	S	L	I
Hill										
Sat	E	L	P	O	E	P	U	S	L	N
Blessed	H	A	P	P	Y	D	S	E	O	T
Happy										
Heart	E	T	R	A	E	H	A	L	W	S
Follower										
Saints	H	E	A	V	E	N	D	B	E	F
Heaven	E	L	B	M	U	H	P	U	R	E
Sad										
Humble										
Pure										

How to

Matthew 5:1-12

Jesus gave a lot of sermons while he lived among us. One of his most famous was called the Sermon on the Mount. In those days Jesus often talked to the people outside, not in church. There were no microphones or pulpits so he just went up on a big hill and sat down. His disciples came and sat down around him. He gave a wonderful sermon. He said, "Happy are the poor in spirit, those who mourn, those who are humble, because they will receive good things from God." Happy are the merciful and the pure in heart, happy are the peacemakers and people who suffer for God's sake — the kingdom of God belongs to them! These must have been happy words for all those folks listening to Jesus. He was helping them to turn sad things into joyful ones.

WORD SCRAMBLE. Try to unscramble these words from today's story.

1. RMONSES
2. ONTUM
3. ISDCILEPS
4. PHAPY
5. DOMKGNI

Be Happy

PUZZLE TIME. The answers to this puzzle can be found in today's lesson. Try to solve it!

Across
1. Today's lesson is all about the _ _ _ _ _ _ on the Mount.
2. Jesus helped the people turn _ _ _ things into joyful ones.
3. Happy are those who suffer for God's sake: the _ _ _ _ _ _ _ belongs to them.
4. Happy are the _ _ _ _ of heart.

Down
4. Happy are the _ _ _ _ in spirit.
5. _ _ _ _ _ gave a lot of sermons when he lived among us.
6. Something that is not crooked is _ _ _ _.
7. Jesus often talked to the people _ _ _ _ _ _ _ instead of in church.
8. When Jesus talked on the mount, the disciples came and sat _ _ _ _ around him.

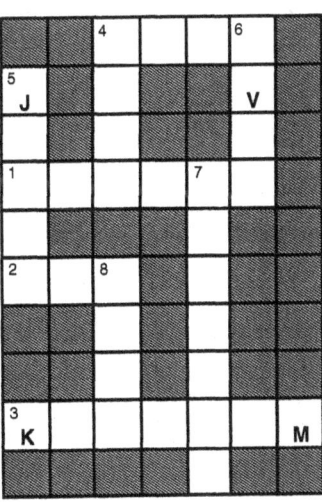

What Flavor

Matthew 5:13-20

Jesus had some very important things to say to us about being Christians. He said that Christians were to be like *salt* for the earth. What does salt do? Sometimes it makes food taste better. It can also keep food from spoiling. Salt is a very important thing. Jesus said that Christians should be like *lights* for the world. They were to let their light shine for others to see. We know that light helps us to find our way in the dark. Lights keep cars from running into each other and help boats find their way into harbor. Christians are to be like salt — full of life — and like light — helping others to see the way to Jesus.

FILL IN THE MISSING WORD. The missing words can be found in today's lesson. Try to fill in the blanks.

1. Today's lesson is all about being a _ _ _ _ _ _ _ _ _.
2. Jesus said we should be like _ _ _ _, full of life for others.
3. Jesus said we should be like _ _ _ _ _, showing the way to Jesus.

Are You?

HIDDEN WORDS. These words are taken from today's lesson. They are hiding in the letters below. You will have to look forward, backward, up, down, and even diagonally to find them. Be sure to circle the ones you find.

Christians							
Taste	C	S	E	E	A	B	C	S
Jesus	H	D	E	F	D	G	H	H
Salt	R	H	T	R	A	E	E	I
See	I	H	H	F	R	T	L	N
Way	S	I	G	O	K	A	P	E
Light	T	A	I	O	L	S	I	F
Dark	I	W	L	D	I	T	N	I
Shine	A	J	A	T	F	E	G	N
Earth	N	K	L	Y	E	M	N	D
Life	S	U	S	E	J	O	R	P
Find								
Food								
Helping								

Make Your Your

Matthew 5:20-37

Did you ever have an argument or a fight with another person? Jesus told us to be very careful about how we treat other people. We shouldn't call anyone names or do other angry things. Jesus said that this is very important. In fact if we come to church to offer our gift to God and remember that someone is angry with us, we should go and first make peace with that person. Then it would be all right to offer our gift to God.

WORD SCRAMBLE. Try to unscramble these mixed up words, then write them in the space provided.

1. SOPERN
2. TTRAE
3. NGRYA
4. EACPE
5. FTIG

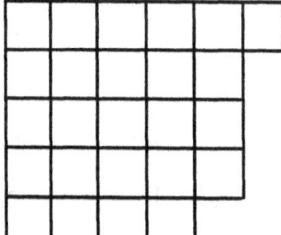

Enemy Friend

PUZZLE TIME. You will find most of the answers to this puzzle in today's lesson. Try to solve it.

Across
1. You should not argue or _ _ _ _ _ with other people.
2. Jesus said we should be _ _ _ _ _ _ _ about how we treat one another.
3. We should try not to be _ _ _ _ _ with others.
4. The Good News of Jesus is called the _ _ _ _ _ _.

Down
2. When we come to _ _ _ _ _ _, we should think about those who are angry with us.
4. We should not offer our _ _ _ _ if we are angry with anyone.
5. Jesus told us many things to help us be _ _ _ _ Christians.
6. How we _ _ _ _ _ our neighbor is very important to God.
7. Before we come to church we should make _ _ _ _ _ with our enemies.
8. _ _ _ _ _ is our best teacher and leader.

Fighting Hate

Matthew 5:38-48

Jesus taught us a lot of things about being Christians. One of his hardest lessons was about how you should treat your enemies. Jesus said: "If someone slaps you on one cheek, let him slap you on the other also! If someone tries to take away your shirt, let him have your coat as well. When a person asks you for something, give it to him. Do not try to get even with your

HIDDEN WORDS. You will find these words hiding in the letters below. Be sure to look up and down, forward and backward, and even diagonally. Circle the ones you find.

Enemies								
Give	E	N	E	M	I	E	S	P	A
Treat	C	G	I	V	E	C	D	E	B
Love									
Cheek	H	O	L	O	V	E	E	R	N
Pray	E	Y	A	R	P	F	G	F	E
Shirt									
Heaven	E	H	I	T	J	K	L	E	V
Perfect									
Coat	K	R	E	W	A	R	D	C	A
Reward	T	A	E	R	T	M	N	T	E
	S	H	I	R	T	O	P	R	H

With Love

enemies — but *love* them. Pray for those who do hurtful things to you." Why should we do all of these difficult things? Because our Father in heaven allows the sun to shine on the good and bad alike. He will not reward us if we love only those people who love us. Jesus said that we should try to be perfect even as our Father in heaven is perfect.

HIDDEN QUESTION. There is a question hiding in the numbers and letters below. Just follow the number one until you form a word. Do the same for all the other numbers until you have the whole question. Write it in the space below. Do you know the answer?

2	9	3	1	5	9	5	4	1
D	E	J	H	U	N	S	T	O
6	9	1	9	7	2	9	3	4
T	E	W	M	T	I	I	E	E
7	3	9	4	7	4	3	6	
R	S	E	L	E	L	U	O	
2	8	7	8	7	9	8	3	
D	O	A	U	T	S	R	S	

Write the question here: _____

Risky

Matthew 10:16-33

One day Jesus sat his disciples down and gave them a good talk about all the things that were going to happen to them. Jesus told them that they would be going out to teach other people about him but it wasn't going to be easy. Sometimes they would be arrested and taken to court. They would be put on trial before kings and other rulers, and this would give them a

PUZZLE TIME. The answers to this puzzle may be found in today's story. Try to solve it.

Across
1. In today's story, Jesus gave his _ _ _ _ _ _ _ _ _ a good talk.
2. Jesus told them of _ _ _ the things that were going to happen to them.
3. Some of the disciples might be _ _ _ _ _ _ _ _ for following Jesus.

Down
1. One _ _ _ Jesus gave his disciples some words of advice.
4. Jesus said that not even one _ _ _ _ of their heads would be lost without God's noticing it.
5. The gospel is the good _ _ _ _ of Jesus.
6. Every hair on each disciple's _ _ _ _ was numbered.
7. Some of Jesus' followers might even have to be on _ _ _ _ _ because of their faith.
8. _ _ _ _ _ told them not to be afraid.
9. Being a disciple of Jesus was not going to be _ _ _ _.
10. The disciples were important to the Father, right down to the _ _ _ _ hair on their heads.

Business

chance to tell others all about the Good News — the gospel. Jesus said that they shouldn't worry about what they would say when they were on trial because the Spirit of the Father would help them out and give them the right words to speak. Most of all, Jesus told his disciples not to be afraid because they were very important to the Father — right down to the very last hair of their heads!

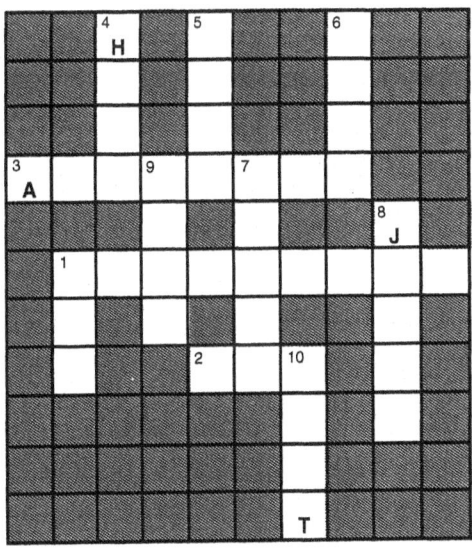

God Loves

Matthew 10:34-42

Jesus was always trying to help his disciples understand what it meant to be his follower. So he talked to them a lot — kind of like a teacher talks to his students. Sometimes they didn't seem to understand what Jesus was saying because it was so different from anything they had heard before.

HIDDEN MESSAGE. A message is hiding for you in the numbers and letters below. Follow the number one until you form a word. Do the same for the rest of the numbers, then write the entire message in the space below.

2	6	3	1	7	4	2	9
S	T	A	J	T	L	P	D
1	8	7	9	5	9	7	1
E	T	E	I	O	S	A	S
9	7	1	8	6	7	1	5
C	C	U	H	I	H	S	F
2	9	4	9	6	7	2	7
E	I	O	P	M	I	N	N
4	9	6	2	9	8	7	9
T	L	E	T	E	E	G	S

Write the message here: _____

Poor People

For example, one time Jesus told them that they would have to take up their cross and follow him if they really wanted to be his disciples. He also said that anyone who would be kind to the poor by giving them something to eat or drink would really be doing that good deed to Jesus! Jesus must have thought that helping out the poor folks was important because he kept reminding his disciples about doing things like that. Wouldn't it have been wonderful to have Jesus for a teacher?

HIDDEN WORDS. These words from today's story are hiding in the letters below. They might be going up, down, forward, backward, or even diagonally. Circle the ones you find.

Follower	F	O	L	L	O	W	E	R	C
Teacher									
Cross	E	C	R	O	S	S	A	B	J
Eat									
Drink	D	A	D	R	A	E	H	D	E
Folks	R	S	T	U	D	E	N	T	S
Students									
Jesus	I	K	R	O	O	P	P	E	U
Poor	N	L	D	E	E	D	L	F	S
Deed									
Good	K	O	G	O	O	D	E	G	H
Heard	A	F	T	E	A	C	H	E	R
Help									

John Was

Matthew 11:2-11

John the Baptizer was never afraid to say what was on his mind. Because of that, he got himself into trouble with King Herod. Herod had John put in prison because of the things John had said about him. Poor John. He must have been feeling pretty gloomy in that prison because one day he sent

HIDDEN WORDS. These words are taken from today's lesson. They are hiding in the letters below. Some are going up or down, forward or backward. You might even find one or two going diagonally. Circle the ones you find.

John	J	O	H	N	X	E	S	W	E	N
Jesus										
Prison	B	A	P	B	E	L	K	C	D	E
Blind										
Good	J	L	R	F	M	B	H	I	G	H
King	E	I	I	J	A	U	E	D	N	K
Lame										
News	S	L	S	N	L	O	R	A	M	G
Trouble	U	G	O	O	D	R	O	E	R	S
Dead										
Happy	S	N	N	O	P	T	D	D	T	U
Herod	L	I	F	E	H	A	P	P	Y	V
Life										

Not Afraid

some of his disciples to Jesus with this question: "Tell us, are you the one John said was going to come, or should we expect someone else?" Jesus sent this message back to John: "... the blind can see, the lame can walk ... the deaf hear, the dead are brought back to life, and the Good News is preached to the poor. How happy are those who have no doubts about me!"

HIDDEN QUESTION. There is a special question for you hiding in the letters and numbers below. Just follow the number one until you form a word. Do the same for two, three, and so on until you find the whole question. Write it in the space provided. Do you know the answer?

1	4	2	3	5	6	7	2	4	5	4	1
W	J	A	D	G	T	J	N	E	I	S	H
7	8	3	5	6	2	1	8	5	9	7	4
O	I	I	V	O	S	A	N	E	P	H	U
9	1	9	2	9	9	3	9	7	2	4	2
R	T	I	W	S	O	D	N	N	E	S	R

Write the question here: _____

A Load You

Matthew 11:25-30

Jesus called many people to follow him. He didn't promise them rich rewards on this earth, like money or power or fame. Most of the time he just told the people that being his follower meant forgetting yourself and thinking mainly of others. This isn't always easy to do but Jesus promised to be a constant helper to his disciples. He said, "Come to me when you are tired from all of your work, and I will give you rest." Jesus also promised his friends that the work he would give them to do — the load he would put on their shoulders — would be light, because he would be right beside them all the time.

WORD SCRAMBLE. These words from today's story got mixed up. Try to straighten them out.

1. OLLOWF
2. ICHR
3. ERHELP
4. MECO
5. STRE
6. DOAL

Can Carry

PUZZLE TIME. You will find the answers to this puzzle in today's story. Try to solve it.

Across
1. Jesus' followers wouldn't always have things like power or _ _ _ _.
2. Jesus said that his burden is _ _ _ _ _.
3. Jesus said that he would be a _ _ _ _ _ _ to his disciples.
4. Just because you follow Jesus you can't expect a rich _ _ _ _ _ _ on this earth.
5. Something you wear on your feet. _ _ _ _
9. The opposite of high. _ _ _

Down
1. Jesus called many people to _ _ _ _ _ _ him.
2. Jesus said that our _ _ _ _ would be easy to carry because he would help us.
6. Jesus carried the cross on his _ _ _ _ _ _ _ _ _.
7. Being a good follower of Jesus means _ _ _ _ _ _ _ _ _ _ yourself.
8. Jesus' followers would not be rewarded on this _ _ _ _ _ but in heaven.

Let It

Matthew 13:1-23

Jesus loved to tell stories so that people would understand him. One day he told a story about a man who went out to plant some seeds in his field. Some of it fell on the path and the birds ate it up. Some of it fell on rocky ground and couldn't grow because there was no soil. Some seed fell in with

HIDDEN MESSAGE. A message is hiding for you in the numbers and letters below. Just follow the number one until you form a word. Do the same for the rest of the numbers, then write the entire message in the space below.

7	8	1	7	6	2	1
T	G	F	O	L	W	A
2	8	9	1	8	6	8
I	O	W	I	D	I	S
1	3	6	2	9	3	1
T	G	S	L	O	R	H
6	2	4	9	3	5	6
T	L	I	R	O	Y	E
3	5	6	4	9	5	
W	O	N	F	D	U	

Write the message here: _____

Grow!

thorn bushes and got all choked up. But some of the seeds fell on good ground and it grew into wonderful plants. Jesus said that this story was really about people and how they listen to God's word. God's word is the seed. Sometimes it falls on people who really don't want to hear it or who are too busy with other things to pay attention. So the seed doesn't grow. But when God's word comes to those who care, then it takes root and blossoms into real, alive faith.

HIDDEN WORDS. These words from today's story are hiding in the letters below. They might be going up or down, forward or backward, or even diagonally. Circle the ones you find.

Seeds	S	E	E	D	S	S	C	P
Field								
Path	S	T	O	R	Y	D	F	L
Birds	R	O	C	K	Y	R	A	A
Soil								
Hear	E	V	I	L	A	I	I	N
Faith								
Good	W	R	W	L	D	B	T	T
Word	O	A	O	P	A	T	H	H
Plant								
Story	R	E	R	G	O	O	D	O
Alive	G	H	D	L	E	I	F	R
Grow								
Listen	A	B	L	I	S	T	E	N
Thorn								
Rocky								

Good and

Matthew 13:24-43

Jesus told a story about a farmer who planted good seed in his field. While he was sleeping, an enemy came and planted weeds among the man's wheat. When the wheat began to grow, so did the weeds, and the poor farmer realized that someone had played a trick on him. Now the farmer didn't want to pull out the weeds right away because he was afraid that he would hurt the wheat, too. So he let the weeds and wheat grow side by side. When the wheat was ready, the farmer had his helpers pull out the weeds, tie them up, and burn them. Then he gathered the wheat into his barn. Jesus said that the wheat and weeds are like good people and bad people who live in this world, side by side. When the final judgment comes, the bad people will be punished and the good people will be taken to live in the Father's house.

FILL IN THE MISSING WORD. Try to fill in the correct word without looking back at today's story.

1. While the farmer was sleeping, an _ _ _ _ _ planted weeds among the man's wheat.
2. The farmer let the wheat and weeds _ _ _ _ side by side.

Bad Together

PUZZLE TIME. You will find the answers to this puzzle in today's story. Try to solve it.

Across
2. The farmer gathered the _ _ _ _ _ into the barn.
5. The farmer was afraid he would _ _ _ _ the wheat if he pulled out the weeds.
6. At the final judgment, the _ _ _ _ people will be taken into the Father's house.
7. On this earth, we all _ _ _ _ together, side by side.
8. At the final judgment the _ _ _ will be separated from the good.

9. In this story, the farmer allowed the wheat and weeds to grow side by _ _ _ _.

Down
1. Today's story is about the final _ _ _ _ _ _ _ _.
2. The farmer allowed the _ _ _ _ _ to grow along with the wheat.
3. Jesus often _ _ _ _ stories or parables to teach the people.
4. Another name for the Father's _ _ _ _ _ is heaven.

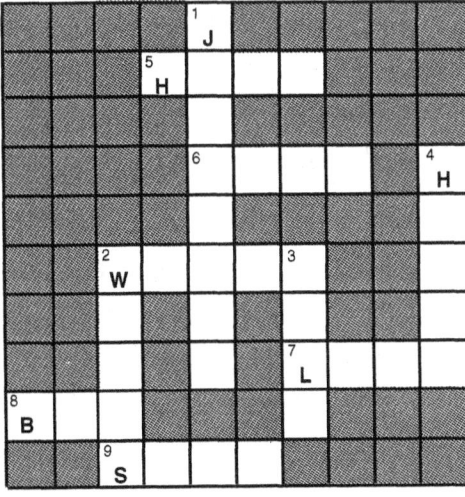

Quick! Sell

Matthew 13:44-52

Jesus wanted to help us understand how wonderful the kingdom of heaven would be. So he told little stories to show us how we should try to get to the kingdom. Jesus said that the kingdom of heaven is like a beautiful treasure hidden in a field. When someone finds it, he goes and gets his money

HIDDEN WORDS. The following words from today's story are hiding in the letters below. They might be going up or down, forward or backward, or even diagonally. Circle the ones you find.

Heaven	H	E	A	V	E	N	S	F
Kingdom	E	K	P	E	A	R	L	I
Treasure								
Field	L	I	E	V	I	G	L	E
Money								
Pearl	P	N	G	B	H	I	E	L
Give	A	G	O	D	U	J	S	D
God								
Sells	B	D	D	E	F	Y	K	L
Buy	N	O	S	R	E	P	M	N
Help								
Person	C	M	O	N	E	Y	O	P
	E	R	U	S	A	E	R	T

Everything!

so he can buy the field. Or, the kingdom of heaven is like the most marvelous pearl in the world. When a person sees it, she sells everything she has just so she can own that pearl. Jesus was trying to tell us that we should be willing to give up everything we have just so we can someday live in God's kingdom of heaven.

HIDDEN MESSAGE. There is a message for you hiding in the letters and numbers below. Just follow the number one until you form a word. Do the same for each of the other numbers. Write the message in the space below.

3	7	5	1	4	6	2	1
I	K	A	T	A	T	S	O

2	8	5	9	6	1	5	8
T	O	B	H	H	D	O	F

1	7	5	2	9	5	2	1
A	I	U	O	E	T	R	Y

4	9	7	2	6	3	4	7
L	A	N	Y	E	S	L	G

1	9	7	9	7	9	7
S	V	D	E	O	N	M

Write the message here: _____

_____

A God-Sized

Matthew 14:13-21

One of the best stories in the Gospel is all about the day that Jesus had a picnic for 5,000 people. He had been preaching to them and it was getting late in the day. The people were far from home and very hungry. So Jesus asked his disciples to give them something to eat. This really upset the disciples because they could only find five loaves of bread and two fish. Well, Jesus took that food, blessed it, and gave thanks to God. He broke the loaves up and asked the disciples to start passing out the bread and fish to the people. Everyone shared in this picnic. When it was over, the disciples took up twelve baskets of leftovers! This was really a picnic to remember.

WORD SCRAMBLE. These words from today's story got mixed up. Try to unscramble them.

1. PSETU
2. SHIF
3. ISCIDPLES
4. NI
5. VEGI
6. CINICP

Picnic

PUZZLE TIME. You will find the answers to this puzzle in today's story. Try to solve it.

Across
1. Jesus had been _ _ _ _ _ _ _ _ _ to the crowds of people.
2. This is the number of baskets of food that the disciples collected after everyone had eaten. _ _ _ _ _ _
3. The people were hungry because it was _ _ _ _ in the day.
4. Jesus blessed five loaves of _ _ _ _ _.
5. There were only two _ _ _ _ to feed all those people.

Down
1. Today's story is about a _ _ _ _ _ _ that Jesus shared with all the people.
6. Everyone who was there had enough to _ _ _.
7. Jesus broke the _ _ _ _ _ _ of bread and passed them out.
8. This word means "on the night before." _ _ _

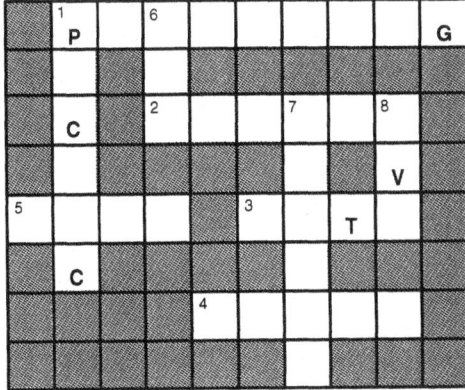

42

A Wild, Weird,

Matthew 14:22-23

One day Jesus wanted to be alone for a while to pray, so he sent the disciples off in their boat. When evening came, the disciples' boat was way out in the middle of the lake. Suddenly a storm blew up with heavy winds that tossed the little boat to and fro. The disciples were afraid. Then they

HIDDEN MESSAGE. A message is hiding in the numbers and letters below. Just follow the number one until you form a word. Do the same for all of the other numbers, then write the entire message on the lines below.

2	7	5	1	8	6	2	1
S	F	B	P	W	H	T	E
7	1	5	8	2	8	5	7
A	T	E	A	A	S	C	I
3	6	5	2	6	4	5	3
T	I	A	R	S	S	U	O
4	1	5	7	4	9	2	5
I	E	S	T	N	W	T	E
1	7	9	2	9	4	2	9
R	H	E	E	A	K	D	K

Write the message here: _____

Watery Walk

saw someone walking toward them on the water! They thought it was a ghost, but then they heard Jesus say, "Don't be afraid. It is I!" Peter immediately had a bright idea. He said, "Lord, if it is really you, tell me to come out on the water, too." Jesus said to him, "Come!" Well, when Peter got out on that water and started walking toward Jesus, he realized what he was doing. Then he started to sink! But Jesus grabbed hold of him and said, "What little faith you have! Why did you doubt?" After that, they both got into the boat and the storm went away.

HIDDEN WORDS. The following words taken from today's story are hiding in the letters below. They might be going up, down, forward, backward, or even diagonally. Circle the ones you find.

Words								
Boat	B	O	A	T	A	B	C	P	D
Pray	L	K	N	I	S	R	H	E	I
Storm									
Lake	P	A	E	F	G	E	H	T	T
Winds	R	J	K	K	L	T	T	E	S
Ghost									
Water	A	I	D	E	A	A	I	R	O
Sink									
Peter	Y	S	D	N	I	W	A	M	H
Faith	S	T	O	R	M	N	F	O	G
Apostles									
Idea	A	P	O	S	T	L	E	S	P

A Good

Matthew 16:13-20

The Apostle Peter didn't always say or do the right thing, but one day he made Jesus very happy with him. Jesus wanted to know what people were saying about him — who they thought he was. The disciples told him that some people thought he was John the Baptist; others thought he was Elijah, Jeremiah, or one of the prophets. Then Jesus asked them, "What about

PUZZLE TIME. You will find the answers to this puzzle in today's story. Try to solve it.

Down
1. John the Baptist was one of the _ _ _ _ _ _ _ _.
2. Today's story is about an important day in the _ _ _ _ of Peter.
3. Jesus asked, "Who do the _ _ _ _ _ _ think I am?"
4. Jesus' disciples _ _ _ _ him what the people were thinking.
5. Peter didn't always do the _ _ _ _ _ thing.
6. _ _ _ _ _ _ _ _ was a prophet who lived before Jesus.
7. Jesus chose twelve disciples who became _ _ _ _ _ _ _ _ to help him with his work.

Across
1. Today's story is about _ _ _ _ _.
8. The disciples were followers of _ _ _ _ _.
9. The opposite of dark. _ _ _ _ _
10. Jesus said that nothing would _ _ _ _ be able to harm the church.
11. Jesus wanted to know what everyone was _ _ _ _ _ _ about him.
12. Jesus was very _ _ _ _ _ _ _ with Peter's answer.

Foundation

you? Who do you think I am?" Peter answered, "You are the Messiah, the Son of the Living God." Jesus was very pleased with Peter. He said, "Good for you, Simon, son of John! This answer came to you from my Father in heaven." Then Jesus told Peter that he would build his church upon his words and that nothing would ever be able to harm it. This was surely one of the most special days in Peter's life!

Talking Like

Matthew 16:21-28

Jesus started telling his disciples about what was going to happen to him some day — that he would go to Jerusalem, suffer, and even die. He also said that three days later he would be raised to life. Well, the disciples didn't like hearing this at all. In fact, Peter took Jesus aside and said to him, "That must never happen to you, Lord!" Those words of Peter made Jesus angry. He told Peter to get away from him because he was talking like the devil instead of like God! Then Jesus told all of his disciples that if they were really going to follow him, they would also have to carry their cross. They would also have to suffer like he was going to suffer. The disciples probably found these words of Jesus very hard to understand.

WORD SCRAMBLE. These words from today's story got all mixed up. Try to unscramble them, then write them in the space provided.

1. SSROC
2. ESJUS
3. IFEL
4. OLLOWF
5. EERTH
6. RAHD

the Devil

HIDDEN WORDS. These words taken from today's story are hiding in the letters below. They might be going up, down, forward, backward, or even diagonally. Circle the ones you find.

Disciples
Die
Follow
Hard
Jesus
Life
Devil
Carry
Words
Suffer
Peter
God
Cross
Three
Days

D	I	S	C	I	P	L	E	S	C	Z
J	I	S	U	F	F	E	R	D	A	W
E	E	E	R	H	T	F	E	R	R	O
S	Y	A	D	A	B	I	T	O	R	A
U	S	S	O	R	C	L	E	W	Y	X
S	G	G	O	D	C	D	P	E	F	E
F	O	L	L	O	W	D	E	V	I	L

47

Mountaintop

Matthew 17:1-9

There is nothing more bright and beautiful than a sunrise or a sunset. The colors are so powerful that a person can't really look at the sun at these times without being blinded. One day Peter, James, and John went with the Lord to a high mountain. There Jesus started to shine — just like a great sunrise or a glowing sunset. The disciples were nearly blinded by the light of Jesus' glory.

PUZZLE TIME. The answers to this puzzle can be found in today's story. Try to solve it.

Across
1. Today we celebrate the day on which _ _ _ _ _ was transfigured.
2. Jesus took the disciples to a _ _ _ _ mountain.
3. In the _ _ _, Jesus glowed like a sunrise.
4. Jesus' clothes were so _ _ _ _ _ _ that the apostles could hardly look at him.
5. The disciples also heard the voice of _ _ _.

Down
4. The disciples were nearly _ _ _ _ _ _ _ by Jesus' glory.
6. _ _ _ _ _, James, and John were allowed to see this wonderful event.
7. All of Jesus' clothes were _ _ _ _ _ _ _.
8. The Father said, "This _ _ my own Dear Son...."

Experience

The Gospel says that Jesus was *"transfigured."* That word means that his whole body changed because the power of God was shining through. These three disciples were certainly lucky to be able to see Jesus in this way. They even heard the voice of the Father saying, "This is my own dear Son, with whom I am pleased — listen to him!"

HIDDEN MESSAGE. There is a message hiding from you in the numbers and letters below. Just follow the number one until you form a word. Do the same for all of the other numbers until you find the whole message. Then write it in the space below.

2	1	7	3	9	1	9	7	3	7	8	9	1
I	T	T	T	J	O	E	R	H	A	O	S	D
7	6	8	2	7	4	1	7	4	9	7	4	9
N	T	F	S	S	F	A	F	E	U	I	S	S
4	7	4	5	7	4	1	7	7	4	3	7	6
T	G	I	O	U	V	Y	R	A	A	E	T	H
7	7	6	4	5	7							
I	O	E	L	F	N							

Write the message here: _____

_____

Forgive

Matthew 18:21-35

Once there was a man whose brother was always doing nasty, mean things to him. Sometimes he would steal his money; other times he would lie to him or call him names. Well, each time something bad happened, the man tried to forgive his brother, but finally one day, the man decided he had had enough. He couldn't forgive him one more time. So he went to church to

PUZZLE TIME. The answers to this puzzle can be found in today's story. Try to solve it!

Across
1. The man in this story had a _ _ _ _ _ brother.
2. This is something we receive when we go to work. _ _ _ _ _
3. This word means that we forgot all of the bad things that someone has done to us. _ _ _ _ _ _ _
4. We are supposed to forgive our neighbor _ _ _ _ _ time he or she does something to hurt us.
5. The opposite of yes. _ _

Down
3. The man in today's story _ _ _ _ _ out what he was supposed to do by listening to the Gospel.
6. This means to tell someone something that isn't true. _ _ _
7. This is the disciple who asked Jesus the question about forgiving his brother. _ _ _ _ _
8. Jesus said we are to forgive our brother _ _ _ _ _ _ _ times seven, which really means always.
9. Another word for nasty is _ _ _ _ _.
10. The disciple _ _ _ _ Jesus for advice about how to treat his brother.
11. The opposite of no. _ _ _

and Forget

find an answer, and there he heard the minister read from the Gospel of Matthew. In that Gospel, Peter comes to Jesus and asks, "Lord, if my brother keeps on sinning against me, how many times do I have to forgive him? Seven times?" Jesus surprised Peter by saying, "Seventy times seven" — which means, forgive him *every* time he does something nasty to you! So the man with the nasty brother found out what he had to do — forgive his brother.

Strange

Matthew 20:1-16

One day Jesus told the people this story. There was a man who needed people to work in his vineyard. So he went out early in the day and found some men who agreed to work for a silver coin; later, he hired another group of men who also agreed to work for him. Then he hired some more men at 12:00, 3:00, and even at 5:00. When evening came, the owner of the

PUZZLE TIME. The answers to this puzzle can be found in today's story. Try to solve it.

Across
1. Jesus told the people many parables — another word for _ _ _ _ _, during his life.
2. In today's story, a man went out and _ _ _ _ _ some people to work for him.
3. The owner of the vineyards _ _ _ _ the men he would pay them fifty dollars.
4. The owner said that he could be _ _ _ _ _ _ _ _ with his money if he wanted to.
5. Jesus said that the first would be _ _ _ _ in the kingdom.

Down
1. The owner agreed to pay the workers a _ _ _ _ _ _ coin.
6. This is a story that Jesus told the _ _ _ _ _ _ who followed.
7. Jesus also said that the last would be _ _ _ _ _ in the kingdom.
8. The owner of the vineyard needed some men to _ _ _ _ for him.
9. The workers who started _ _ _ _ _ got the same pay as those who came later.

Generosity

vineyard called those who were hired at 5:00 and paid them a silver coin. When those who had worked all day heard this, they grumbled because they thought they should get more money. But the owner said, "I haven't cheated you. You agreed to work for a silver coin and that's what I've given you. Can't I be generous if I want to?" Jesus told the people that in the kingdom of heaven those who are last will be first and those who are first will be last.

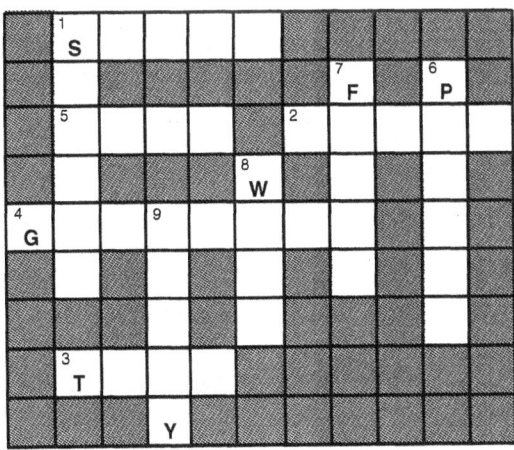

Time For

Matthew 21:1-11

Do you remember the day called Palm Sunday by many Christians throughout the world? Well, one day as Jesus and his disciples were going toward Jerusalem, Jesus asked his disciples to bring him a donkey which they would find in the village ahead. The disciples did what Jesus asked and brought the donkey back to him. Jesus got on it and rode into Jerusalem. As

PUZZLE TIME. All of the answers to this puzzle can be found in today's story. Try to solve it.

Across
1. Today is sometimes called _ _ _ _ Sunday.
2. On this day _ _ _ _ _ led the parade to Jerusalem.
3. Jesus _ _ _ _ to Jerusalem, but everyone else walked.
4. The people picked up _ _ _ _ _ _ _ _ to wave.
5. "_ _ _ of David" was a title given to Jesus.
6. Many people came to _ _ _ Jesus on this day.
7. The people kept shouting, "_ _ _ _ _ _ to the Son of David!"

Down
8. Jesus asked his disciples to bring him a _ _ _ _ _ _ to ride on.
9. This was the city where Jesus was going. _ _ _ _ _ _ _ _ _
10. People who follow Christ are called _ _ _ _ _ _ _ _ _ _.

a Parade

Jesus went along, a large crowd of people gathered. They spread their cloaks before him. They picked up palm branches and started waving them and shouting, "Praise to the Son of David! God bless him who comes in the name of the Lord!" It must have been just like a parade, with Jesus leading the way on his donkey. All the people in Jerusalem wondered who this strange man could be. The crowds who followed Jesus told them: "This is the prophet Jesus from Nazareth in Galilee."

The Angry

Matthew 21:33-43

Jesus told the people this story to help them understand the Kingdom of God. Once there was a man who planted a vineyard. When he had it all ready, he rented it to some people and then went on a trip. When it was time to gather the grapes, the owner sent his servants to get the grapes that belonged to him. But the renters wouldn't give the servants any of the grapes.

HIDDEN WORDS. These words are hiding in the letters below. All of them were taken from today's story. You might find these words going up or down, forward or backward, or even diagonally. Circle the ones you find.

People
Story
Kingdom
God
Planted
Rented
Trip
Grapes
Sent
Servants
Son
Father
Gift

P	E	O	P	L	E	A	F
L	Y	R	O	T	S	K	A
A	D	S	E	N	T	I	T
N	O	S	B	C	D	N	H
T	G	I	F	T	E	G	E
E	R	E	N	T	E	D	R
D	F	I	G	H	I	O	J
G	R	A	P	E	S	M	K
S	E	R	V	A	N	T	S

Landlord

Instead, they threw them out. Then the owner sent his son to get the money and the grapes that belonged to his father. This time, the renters grabbed the son and killed him. When the people heard this story, they agreed that the owner should come and punish the renters, throw them out of the vineyard, and give the vineyard to other people who could be trusted. Jesus told this story to help the people understand how they were treating the Father's gift to them — Jesus.

HIDDEN MESSAGE. There is a message for you hiding in the numbers and letters below. If you want to find it, just follow the number one until you form the first word. Do the same for each of the other numbers until you have the whole message. Then write it in the space below.

2	1	6	4	3	1	6	4	7
W	J	T	F	T	E	O	A	U
8	2	9	5	3	1	4	2	7
H	A	P	G	H	S	T	S	S
1	4	5	8	4	9	8	4	3
U	H	I	I	E	E	S	R	E
9	1	5	9	4	5	9	9	
O	S	F	P	S	T	L	E	

Write the message here: _____

The Big

Matthew 25:31-46

Jesus told us what it would be like on Judgment Day. The Son of Man would come with all the angels, and he would divide the people into two groups. Those who have answered God's call will be on his right. To them he will say, "Come and enjoy the kingdom. I was hungry and you fed me;

PUZZLE TIME. You can find all of the answers to this puzzle in today's story. Try to solve it!

Across
1. Today's story is about _ _ _ _ _ _ _ _ Day.
2. Jesus will _ _ _ to those on his right, "Come and enjoy the kingdom."
3. When you visit the _ _ _ _, those who are ill, you are doing the Lord's work.
4. The people who answered God's call will be on his _ _ _ _ _.
5. Jesus said, "I was _ _ _ _ _ and you clothed me."
6. Jesus said, "I was _ _ _ _ _ _ and you fed me."
7. On the last day the _ _ _ of Man will come to judge the world.
8. Our _ _ _ _ _ is the part of us that will go on living, even after we die.

Down
1. The person who talked to the people about Judgment Day was _ _ _ _ _.
3. A person whom nobody knows is a _ _ _ _ _ _ _ _, someone the Lord said to welcome into our homes.
9. God wants all of us to _ _ _ _ _ the kingdom.
10. These will come with Jesus when he arrives to judge the world. _ _ _ _ _ _

Surprise

thirsty, and you gave me a drink; I was a stranger and you took me into your homes; I was naked and you clothed me; I was sick and you took care of me; I was in prison and you visited me." Then the people will say, "Lord, when did we do these good things for you?" And the Lord will answer, "Whenever you did these things for one of the least of my brothers and sisters, you did it for me!"

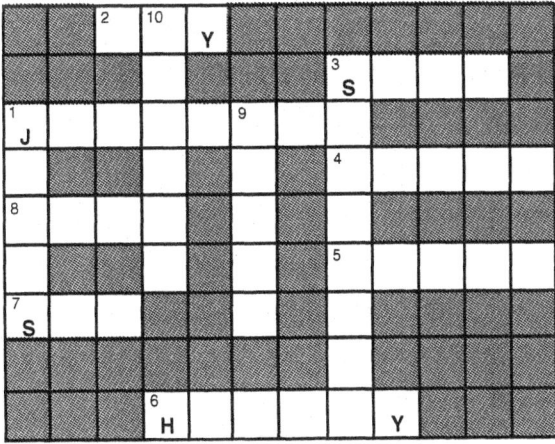

When "No" Means "Yes"

Matthew 21:28-32

Jesus told a story about a man who had two sons. One day he went to the older son and asked him to go and work in the vineyard. But the son didn't want to, so he said, "No." Later, the son changed his mind and went to the vineyard to work.

Then the father asked his younger son to work in the vineyard. This son immediately said he would go, but he never did show up at the vineyard. Jesus asked the people, "Which son did what the father wanted him to do?" They answered, "The older one." Then Jesus told them that they had better follow the path of John the Baptist or they would not get to heaven. They would be like the younger son who said one thing but did another.

WORD SCRAMBLE. These words from today's story got all mixed up. Try to straighten them out, then write them in the space provided.

1. ONSS
2. YAD
3. INDM
4. ATHFER
5. THAP
6. EAVHEN

www.ingramcontent.com/pod-product-compliance
Lightning Source LLC
Chambersburg PA
CBHW071758040426
42446CB00012B/2606